I0465435

MASTER THE CRAFT OF POWERFUL SPEAKING

The Secrets to Captivating Audiences, Delivering Impactful Messages and Speaking with Authority and Influence.

SOPHIA EVERLY

1

Copyright © George C. Scott, 2024.

SOPHIA EVERLY

SOPHIA EVERLY

Introduction:

Why Mastering Public Speaking Matters

In today's world, effective public speaking is a crucial skill. Whether you are addressing a group of professionals, delivering a speech at a wedding, or simply presenting your ideas to colleagues, your ability to communicate effectively can significantly impact your success. Yet,

SOPHIA EVERLY

many people fear public speaking more than any other form of social interaction.

Mastering public speaking allows you to express your thoughts clearly, influence others, and build confidence. It's not only the content of your message that matters but also the way you deliver it. When done right, public speaking can lead to opportunities, relationships, and even leadership positions.

In this book, you will learn not just how to overcome the fear of public speaking but how to excel in it. From overcoming stage fright to engaging your audience, you'll acquire the skills to speak confidently and leave a lasting impression.

SOPHIA EVERLY

Chapter 1: Overcoming Stage Fright

One of the most common challenges people face in public speaking is stage fright. It's natural to feel nervous before stepping in front of an audience, but the key is to manage that nervousness and turn it into energy that enhances your presentation.

What Causes Stage Fright?

Stage fright often stems from a fear of judgment or making mistakes. The idea of being the center of attention can be overwhelming, especially if you're worried about forgetting what to say or facing an uninterested audience. This fear triggers the body's "fight or flight" response, leading to symptoms like sweating, shaking, or a dry mouth.

How to Manage Stage Fright

Prepare Thoroughly

SOPHIA EVERLY

The more thoroughly you prepare, the more confident you'll become. Rehearse your speech several times until you feel fully comfortable with the content. Familiarity reduces anxiety.

Visualize Success

Before stepping on stage, take a moment to visualize yourself delivering the speech successfully. Imagine the audience responding positively, applauding, and engaging with you. Visualization is a powerful tool used by athletes and performers to build confidence.

Focus on Breathing

Deep, controlled breathing helps calm your nerves. Before speaking, take slow, deep breaths to lower your heart rate and clear your mind. Even during your speech, if you feel anxious, pausing for a deep breath can help center you.

Turn Nervousness into Excitement

Studies show that nervousness and excitement are similar physiological responses. By reframing your nervousness as excitement, you can turn that energy into enthusiasm. Rather than telling yourself, "I'm nervous," try reframing it as, "I'm excited to share this!"

SOPHIA EVERLY

Engage with Your Audience Early

Breaking the ice early on can make you feel more connected with your audience and reduce the feeling of isolation that often leads to stage fright. Start with a light joke, a question, or a relatable story to create rapport.

Practice Exercise:

Mirror Speaking: Stand in front of a mirror and deliver your speech as if you were speaking to an audience. This helps you become comfortable with your gestures, facial expressions, and overall delivery.

Record and Review: Record yourself delivering the speech, then watch the playback to identify areas for improvement. This will also help you get used to seeing yourself perform, making the actual event less intimidating.

Stage fright is a natural response, but it doesn't have to hold you back. With preparation, visualization, and techniques to manage anxiety, you can transform your nervous energy into powerful, confident public speaking.

SOPHIA EVERLY

Chapter 2: The Art of Persuasion

Effective public speaking isn't just about conveying information; it's about persuading your audience to believe in your message. Whether you're selling a product, advocating for a cause, or inspiring others, the ability to persuade is key to success.

Understanding Persuasion

Persuasion involves influencing your audience by appealing to their emotions, values, and logic. Aristotle's classic model of persuasion—ethos, pathos, and logos—remains just as relevant today.

Ethos refers to your credibility. Audiences are more likely to listen to speakers they trust and respect.

Pathos is the emotional appeal. Stories, metaphors, and anecdotes can tug at heartstrings, making your message more relatable.

Logos refers to logic and reasoning. A well-structured argument with solid evidence ensures that your audience can follow your reasoning.

SOPHIA EVERLY

Techniques for Persuasive Speaking

Know Your Audience

Understanding your audience's values, needs, and beliefs allows you to tailor your message effectively. Research your audience beforehand to find out what motivates them.

Use Compelling Stories

People remember stories more than statistics. A personal anecdote or case study that reinforces your point can have a profound impact on how your message is received.

Be Authentic

Authenticity builds trust. Speak from your own experiences and beliefs, and your audience will sense your sincerity. People are more likely to be persuaded when they believe the speaker is genuine.

Appeal to Emotions

Emotions drive decisions. To persuade, touch on emotions such as fear, hope, joy, or empathy. However, avoid manipulating

SOPHIA EVERLY

emotions—focus on connecting them to the core message of your speech.

SOPHIA EVERLY

Provide Solid Evidence

Persuasion is most effective when it's backed by facts. Use data, expert opinions, and research to support your argument. Ensure that your evidence is accurate and reliable, as your credibility hinges on the quality of your information.

Practice Exercise:

Craft a Persuasive Argument: Pick a topic you are passionate about. Write a persuasive argument using ethos, pathos, and logos. Practice delivering this argument to a friend or in front of a mirror, focusing on how you can connect with your audience.

Mastering the art of persuasion requires a balance between emotion, credibility, and logic. By using these techniques, you can influence your audience's thoughts and actions, making your message more impactful.

SOPHIA EVERLY

Chapter 3: Building a Strong Presence

A commanding stage presence can make or break a presentation. Regardless of your content, if you don't engage your audience with your energy, confidence, and body language, your message may be lost.

What Is Presence?

Presence is the way you project yourself when you speak. It's not only about what you say, but how you say it that matters. When you have a strong presence, you exude confidence, even if you feel nervous inside.

Tips for Building Presence

Confidence in Posture

Stand tall, shoulders back, and head held high. A powerful stance not only makes you look confident but also makes you feel more confident. Avoid slouching or pacing excessively, which can undermine your authority.

Eye Contact

SOPHIA EVERLY

Making eye contact helps create a strong connection with your audience. Rather than looking over your audience, focus on different individuals throughout the room, making them feel engaged and involved in your presentation.

Controlled Gestures

Your hands can be powerful tools when used effectively. Use gestures to emphasize key points, but be mindful of overuse, which can be distracting. Open, expansive gestures suggest confidence, while crossed arms or fidgeting can signal nervousness.

Voice Control

A commanding voice grabs attention. Practice varying your tone, pitch, and volume to avoid a monotone delivery. Pausing at strategic moments can add drama or allow your audience time to absorb key points.

Movement with Purpose

Moving around the stage can energize your audience, but it must be purposeful. Avoid aimless pacing, which can be distracting. Use movement to emphasize transitions in your speech or to connect with different parts of the audience.

SOPHIA EVERLY

Practice Exercise:

Record Yourself Speaking: Focus on your body language and vocal delivery. Are you maintaining good posture? Are your gestures natural? Analyze the recording and adjust your presence accordingly.

Building a strong presence is essential to captivating your audience. By focusing on your body language, voice, and movement, you'll appear confident and engaging, leaving a lasting impression on your listeners.

Chapter 4: Crafting Memorable Messages

A memorable message is the cornerstone of great public speaking. Even if your delivery is perfect, your audience won't remember your speech unless your content is structured in a compelling and digestible way.

SOPHIA EVERLY

The Power of Structure

One of the keys to making your message memorable is organizing your speech effectively. Audiences tend to remember information better when it's presented in a clear, structured format.

Three-Part Structure

Introduction: Hook your audience with an intriguing fact, a powerful question, or a personal story. Provide your audience with a reason to be interested in your topic.

Body: Break down your message into three to five key points. Support each point with evidence, examples, and anecdotes.

Conclusion: Summarize your main points and leave the audience with a strong final thought or call to action.

Tips for Memorable Content

Simplicity Is Key

Avoid overwhelming your audience with too much information. Focus on one core message and ensure that everything in your speech supports that message.

SOPHIA EVERLY

Use Repetition

Repetition reinforces your message. Key phrases or ideas repeated throughout your speech will stick in the audience's mind.

Create Visuals in Their Minds

Use descriptive language to paint vivid pictures. When your audience can "see" what you're talking about, they're more likely to remember it.

End with a Bang

The conclusion of your speech is often what leaves the strongest impression on your audience. Make sure it's powerful, whether it's a quote, a story, or a challenge.

Practice Exercise:

Craft a Speech Outline: Write an outline for a speech using the three-part structure. Focus on a clear message and ensure that each section flows logically into the next.

Crafting a memorable message is about simplicity, structure, and impact. By organizing your speech effectively and using vivid, memorable language, you'll leave a lasting impression on your audience.

SOPHIA EVERLY

Chapter 5: Audience Engagement Techniques

A great public speaker doesn't just deliver a monologue—they create a dialogue, even in a large auditorium. Engaging your audience is the key to holding their attention, making your message resonate, and ensuring that they stay with you from start to finish.

Why Audience Engagement Matters

When your audience is engaged, they're more likely to remember your message, respond positively, and even act on your call to action. Engagement isn't just about keeping people awake; it's about creating a connection that makes your speech more impactful.

Techniques for Engaging Your Audience

Start with a Question

SOPHIA EVERLY

Opening with a question immediately engages your audience by prompting them to think. This could be a rhetorical question to provoke thought or a direct question to encourage interaction. For instance, you could ask, "Who here has ever felt anxious before a major presentation?"

Use Humor Strategically

Humor can ease tension and help you appear more relatable to your audience. A well-placed joke or light-hearted comment can help relax both you and your audience. However, be careful with humor—ensure it's appropriate for your audience and the setting.

Invite Participation

Direct interaction helps maintain attention. Ask for a show of hands or invite audience members to share their thoughts or experiences. When people feel involved, they're more likely to stay engaged.

Tell Relatable Stories

Personal stories or anecdotes that your audience can relate to will keep them emotionally connected to your message. The more your audience can relate to your stories, the more invested they will become.

Vary Your Tone and Pace

SOPHIA EVERLY

A monotone delivery can cause your audience's attention to drift. Use vocal variety to maintain interest—change your tone, pitch, and volume throughout your speech. Similarly, varying the pace of your delivery keeps your audience on their toes.

Use Visual Aids Effectively

Visual aids such as slides, props, or demonstrations can make your message more tangible and easier to follow. However, make sure the visuals complement your message rather than distract from it. Keep slides simple, and don't overload them with text.

Pose Hypothetical Scenarios

Create "what if" scenarios that encourage your audience to imagine themselves in a certain situation. For example, "Imagine you're standing in front of a large crowd, ready to deliver the most important speech of your career. What's the first thing you do?"

Encourage Active Listening

A simple way to engage your audience is to ask them to reflect on your key points. For instance, after discussing a key idea, ask them, "Take a moment to think about how this applies to your own life."

SOPHIA EVERLY

Overcoming Audience Apathy

Sometimes, no matter how engaging you try to be, your audience may seem uninterested. This could be due to external factors like a long event or a topic they're not initially passionate about. When faced with a disengaged audience:

Acknowledge the Situation: Sometimes, simply recognizing that your audience might be tired or distracted helps reset the energy. You could say something like, "I know it's been a long day, but stick with me for just a few more minutes".

Change the Energy: Use a change in tone, an unexpected joke, or a shift in your presentation style to jolt the audience back to attention.

Involve a Volunteer: Bringing someone from the audience up to the stage for a demonstration or discussion can re-engage everyone.

Practice Exercise:

Interactive Practice: Write a section of your speech where you deliberately ask for audience interaction, whether through a question, a call for participation, or a show of hands. Practice delivering this with a group to see how they respond.

Engaging your audience is essential to delivering a powerful and memorable speech. By asking questions, inviting participation, using humor, and telling relatable stories, you can create a twoway connection that makes your presentation more dynamic and impactful.

SOPHIA EVERLY

SOPHIA EVERLY

Chapter 6: Handling Difficult Questions

Every public speaker will, at some point, face challenging questions from the audience. Whether these questions are genuinely inquisitive or intended to provoke, how you respond can either enhance your credibility or diminish your authority. Handling difficult questions with confidence and poise is an essential skill for mastering the art of public speaking.

Why Questions Can Be Challenging

Difficult questions may come in various forms. Some might challenge your expertise, while others could seem irrelevant or antagonistic. Regardless of their intent, how you respond says a lot about your composure, preparation, and ability to think on your feet.

Strategies for Handling Tough Questions

Stay Calm and Composed

SOPHIA EVERLY

The first rule of handling tough questions is to remain calm. If a question catches you off guard, take a deep breath and pause for a moment before responding. Avoid reacting defensively, as this can make you appear flustered or insecure.

Clarify the Question

If a question is unclear, ask the person to rephrase it or provide more context. This gives you time to think and ensures that you understand exactly what they're asking before you respond. For example, "Could you clarify what you mean by that?" or "Are you asking about X or Y?"

Acknowledge Valid Points

If the question raises a legitimate concern or viewpoint, acknowledge it before offering your response. This shows that you respect the person's input and are open to differing perspectives. For instance, "That's a great point, and I understand why you might see it that way."

Buy Time with a Thoughtful Pause

If you need a moment to collect your thoughts, don't be afraid to take a brief pause. This not only gives you time to form a coherent

SOPHIA EVERLY

response but also demonstrates that you're taking the question seriously. You can also use phrases like, "That's an interesting question—let me think about that for a moment."

Answer Honestly

If you're unsure of the answer to a question, it's best to acknowledge it honestly. Pretending to know something when you don't can damage your credibility. Instead, acknowledge the question and offer to follow up later. For example, "I don't have the answer to that off the top of my head, but I'd be happy to look into it and get back to you."

Defuse Hostility

If a question seems hostile or accusatory, don't respond with hostility. A calm and measured response can defuse tension. Acknowledge the question without being defensive. For instance, you might say, "I understand your perspective and value your honesty". Let me explain my perspective."

Redirect Off-Topic Questions

Sometimes, audience members will ask questions that are offtopic or irrelevant to the discussion. Politely acknowledge the question but steer the conversation back to the main topic. For example, you could say, "That's a significant issue, but it's a bit outside the focus of our discussion today". I'd be happy to address it afterward."

SOPHIA EVERLY

27

SOPHIA EVERLY

Involve the Audience

If you're stumped by a particularly tough question, don't hesitate to involve the audience. Ask if anyone else has insights or suggestions. This approach not only shows humility but also encourages audience participation. For example, "That's a tricky question—does anyone else have thoughts on this?"

Handling Question and Answer Sessions Effectively

When giving a formal presentation, a Q&A session is often part of the program. Managing this portion effectively can further enhance your credibility.

- *Set the Tone:* At the beginning of the Q&A, set the expectation that you will answer questions to the best of your ability and encourage respectful dialogue.
- *Limit Response Time:* If a question requires a lengthy explanation, summarize your response to avoid losing the audience's attention.
- *Prepare for Common Questions:* Anticipate questions based on your topic and prepare responses ahead of time.
   This reduces the chances of being caught off guard.

SOPHIA EVERLY

Practice Exercise:

Simulate a Q&A: Have a friend or colleague play the role of an audience member and ask you difficult or unexpected questions. Practice responding calmly and effectively, even when faced with tough questions.

Handling difficult questions is a crucial skill for any public speaker. By staying calm, clarifying questions, and responding with honesty and poise, you can navigate even the most challenging moments with confidence. Remember, your goal is not to have all the answers but to engage thoughtfully and respectfully with your audience.

Chapter 7: Using Technology to Enhance Presentations

In today's world, technology plays a vital role in public speaking. Whether you're delivering a business presentation, a lecture, or a keynote speech, using technology effectively can amplify your message and engage your audience in ways that words alone cannot. However, when misused, technology can become a distraction that takes away from your core message.

The Role of Technology in Public Speaking

Technology is a tool to enhance your presentation, not replace it. Visual aids, slides, and multimedia should support your message by providing clarity, emphasis, and engagement. When used thoughtfully, they can help your audience understand complex information and make your speech more memorable.

Choosing the Right Tools

With so many technological options available, it's important to select the right tools for your specific presentation. Here are some commonly used technologies in public speaking:

Presentation Software *(e.g., PowerPoint, Keynote, Google Slides)*

Slide presentations are one of the most popular tools in public speaking. They allow you to display key points, images, charts, and videos that complement your speech. However, it's crucial to keep slides simple and clean—too much text or cluttered visuals can overwhelm your audience.

SOPHIA EVERLY

Multimedia *(Videos, Audio Clips)*

Adding a short video or audio clip can break up your presentation and offer a different medium for communicating your message. For example, a video testimonial can be more impactful than simply quoting someone. Be sure the multimedia is relevant and concise to avoid losing your audience's focus.

Interactive Tools *(Polls, Quizzes, Q&A Platforms)*

Online tools such as live polling apps or interactive quizzes can engage your audience by making them active participants. Tools like **Mentimeter** or **Slido** allow audiences to submit questions or participate in live polls, providing real-time feedback and making your presentation more dynamic.

Visual Aids *(Charts, Graphs, Infographics)*

Using visual aids to represent data or concepts can make complex information easier to understand. Instead of simply describing.... Rather than talking through numbers or statistics, showing a well-designed chart or infographic can make data easier to digest. Use visuals sparingly, ensuring that they serve a clear purpose.

SOPHIA EVERLY

Best Practices for Using Technology

To ensure technology enhances your presentation without distracting from your message, follow these best practices:

Keep Slides Simple and Visual

Slides should reinforce what you're saying, not repeat it word-forword. Use bullet points to summarize key ideas and limit each slide to one main concept. Visuals such as images or icons can be more powerful than text. Aim for a clean and uncluttered design with minimal text—your audience should be listening to you, not reading off the screen.

Practice with Your Technology

Familiarize yourself with the technology you'll be using. Run through your slides or multimedia ahead of time to ensure everything works smoothly. Technology glitches can throw off your presentation, so practice with the actual equipment and room setup if possible. This also includes having a backup plan in case of technical failures.

Don't Overuse Multimedia

While multimedia can enhance a presentation, using too much can overwhelm or distract your audience. For example, showing multiple videos or relying heavily on sound effects might take the focus away from your speech. Use multimedia selectively to support your core points.

Engage with the Audience, Not the Screen

Don't fall into the trap of constantly looking at your slides instead of your audience. Maintain eye contact and engage with the people in the room. Your slides or visuals are there to supplement your message, but your connection with the audience is the priority.

Ensure Technology Supports Your Message

The purpose of technology is to enhance the understanding of your message. Always ask yourself whether a visual or multimedia element adds value to your presentation. If it doesn't contribute to clarifying or emphasizing your point, it's best to leave it out.

Test the Venue's Equipment

If you're speaking at a venue that provides equipment, arrive early to test everything. Check the projector, sound system, and internet connection (if needed). You don't want to encounter technical issues during your presentation that could have been avoided with a quick run-through.

SOPHIA EVERLY

Interactive Elements: Keeping the Audience Involved

Interactive technology allows you to break the barrier between speaker and audience, encouraging real-time feedback and participation. For example:

- **Live Polls:** Ask your audience to vote on a question or share their opinions using a polling tool. Display the results instantly to discuss them and create an engaging dialogue.
- **Q&A Platforms:** Encourage your audience to ask questions throughout the presentation using platforms like Slido. You can then address the most popular or relevant questions in real-time.
- **Interactive Quizzes:** Test your audience's knowledge or understanding of key concepts with quick quizzes. This can make your presentation more engaging and help reinforce important points.

Examples of Technology in Action

Data-Driven Presentations

A speaker presenting on the benefits of renewable energy might use charts and graphs to show changes in global energy consumption over time. Visual data helps the audience grasp the scale of change more easily than verbal explanation alone.

SOPHIA EVERLY

Engaging Keynote Speeches

A motivational speaker might use video clips of personal stories or impactful moments to illustrate key themes, helping the audience connect emotionally.

Workshops and Training Sessions

For interactive workshops, tools like digital whiteboards or live collaboration platforms (e.g., Miro) can help the audience participate more actively, whether remotely or in person.

Practice Exercise:

Create a Slide Presentation: Design a short slide deck using the principles of simplicity and clarity. Focus on creating visually engaging slides that complement your speech, avoiding clutter and excessive text.

Technology is a powerful tool that, when used effectively, can elevate your public speaking. Whether through slide presentations, multimedia, or interactive elements, technology can enhance your message and engage your audience. However, the key is to use it thoughtfully, ensuring that it supports rather than overshadows your content.

SOPHIA EVERLY

Conclusion:

Final Thoughts and Encouragement

Public speaking is both an art and a science. Mastering the act of public speaking requires practice, self-awareness, and a willingness to continuously improve. Throughout this book, you've learned techniques for overcoming fear, engaging your audience, crafting persuasive messages, and using technology to enhance your presentations.

But the most important lesson is this: public speaking is a skill that anyone can develop. No matter where you start, with dedication and practice, you can become a confident, effective speaker who makes an impact every time you step in front of an audience.

As you continue on your journey, remember:

Preparation is essential: the more you rehearse, the more confidence you will gain.

SOPHIA EVERLY

Engage your audience: Build a connection with them to keep their attention and make your message resonate.

Embrace challenges: Whether it's handling difficult questions or unexpected technical issues, stay calm and composed.

Always be authentic: Your voice, your experiences, and your passion are what make you stand out.

Now, it's time to take what you've learned and apply it. Go out there, speak with confidence, and leave a lasting impact on your audience.

SOPHIA EVERLY